I0052965

THE BOOK OF BRANDING

A Christian's Guide to SUCCESSFULLY Creating and Marketing a Business

———

Ty B. McKenzie

THE BOOK OF BRANDING
Copyright © 2015 by Ty B. McKenzie

All rights reserved. No part of this book may be reproduced or transmitted in any form or by any means without written permission from the author.

ISBN **978-0-9861989-0-8**

Printed in USA.

I am eternally grateful to God for the opportunity to share my words with the world. God, I thank you for life, salvation and creativity.

I pray you are blessed by this book
and are encouraged to
BE BOLD, BE EXCELLENT, BE THE BRAND!

Table of Contents

Foreword

One of the new modern day terms we hear in this ever-changing field of marketing is the term "branding". Whether it is a person's name or their business, the desire to be known by a certain message or ideal is the new trend. While this concept appears to be new, in reality it is as ancient as biblical days. When God would speak to His people concerning His character and His names as they related to His nature, it was branding. When Jesus asked the disciples who people said that He was and followed it up with asking THEM who He was, it was not as simple as a question of His name or identity. It was a question of how persons saw Him based on His action in ministry. Jesus was concerned about His branding. While branding is a term and a practice that is seen most often in the corporate world, it is refreshing when corporate concepts are retooled with Christian concepts.

That is what I love about this book by Ty McKenzie. As you read this book, you will discover the thoughts and practices of a young lady who has established herself as a businesswoman who marches to Kingdom principles. If you are in ministry in the church, para-church or the marketplace, this book is a must read for understanding the necessity of branding and how to do it in a way that shows forth your witness of Christ. I speak this not only as one who knows the author but also as one who is a client of the author. Be careful...when you read this book, you just might become one as well.

Bishop Rudolph W. McKissick, Jr.

From the Author

If you are reading this right now then I am sure you have felt (or currently feel) several emotions regarding your business or brand. Allow me to name a few of them. Excited. Anxious. Disappointed. Frustrated. Overwhelmed by the process. Underwhelmed by the progress. Happy. Confused. Elated. All of the above. Repeat cycle. Sound familiar? Let me help you deal with that right now. That emotional chaos is totally understandable, expected and normal. Every successful entrepreneur has faced those feelings. The important thing to remember is to battle through the tough moments and refuse to get stuck there. It is my hope that at the end of this book you will be empowered to take on the task of growing your business. The job may be tough but it is possible with the proper tools and practices in place. Get ready to put in the hard work and transform your image. It is time to elevate your brand and go to the next level!

P.S. I love hearing your success stories! After you finish the book, email me ty@elevatyd.com and let me know how this guide has helped you!

Peace, blessings and success,

Ty B. McKenzie

Introduction

Before we get into the content I want to share five simple reasons why you marketing efforts are not working to build your brand. Think of this as the appetizer for your meal. Keep these points in mind as we go talk through this entire book. By the time you finish this book, I want you to feel empowered and enabled to build the best brand you can.

IDENTITY

Your brand has no clear identity.

What is your logo? What does your branding package look like? It is essential to remember that people are visual beings. We subconsciously associate feelings, memories and emotions to objects and colors. Without any effort you can easily associate the brand behind the golden arches. McDonald's and every other successful brand realize the importance of knowing and sticking with your identity. Your look should be consistent. The customer should be able to recognize your brand through visual elements that are used on a regular basis. For example, if you are hosting an event but have seven different flyers that have three different logos, expect your customers to be confused. Confusion is NOT what you want! Every good idea you have does not belong in a single campaign. When in doubt, keep it simple to be sure that your message and identity are clearly communicated.

VISION

You have no idea what the end should look like.

Do you have a marketing plan? Your business should have a marketing plan. Your new product launch should have a marketing plan. Your company's grand opening should have a marketing plan. Did you see the trend? Before you start doing ANYTHING related to marketing, you need to plan it out. It is easier to stay on track when the plan is clearly laid out. When a marketing plan is present it provides a measure to gauge whether or not a campaign was successful.

DIVERSITY

You rely on one source of marketing for your brand's success.

This one is very important! You CANNOT rely on one outlet for all of your marketing needs. I am a believer in the power of social media. Creating a Facebook event and posting your flyer several times per day is not the key to having a great event. The audience you are trying to reach may not connect with that type of marketing. I have seen many clients come to me in frustration because they have posted advertisements every hour on their Facebook page and it has not yielded any results. A TV commercial may be more appropriate for the situation but remember to consider the station and airplay times. A radio ad during morning and afternoon drive times may be it for you. Internet ads through Google Adwords or a billboard on a major highway may be what you need. Perhaps you need all of them! Just remember to broaden your net.

VALUE

You think marketing isn't necessary.

This is the MOST IMPORTANT point! Small business owners are often guilty of allocating budgets for everything except marketing. It does not matter how amazing the product and packaging are if there is no plan or budget to tell your customers about it. Invest in the graphic designer to create the flyers, billboards and additional collateral. Invest in the marketing consultant to help you identify the proper channels to use. Invest in the radio ads, TV commercials, social media ads and more. Remember that it is an investment.

TARGETING

You don't know who you should market to.

I won't spend too much time on this one since we will discuss it more in detail. This element will be figured out in the marketing plan creation process. Always think about your customer. Learn everything you can about them before speaking to them and asking them to purchase anything from you.

Let's get into the main course!

SECTION ONE

What's your excuse? Write it down below.

_____

_____

This is the last time we will mention it. No
excuses are allowed here.

Chapter One

One of the most dangerous mistakes a person can make on the road to success is to refuse guidance. Learning is an essential key to greatness. While most people spend a small portion of their lives in a traditional educational system, knowledge should continue throughout your entire lifespan. Creating a plan for continuing education is necessary to becoming an industry leader. You must have an understanding of your area before you can become a master within it. I know this may seem like an unexpected step in the branding process but trust me it is an important one.

Find out what the common certifications are within your industry. Education does not end with high school, college or graduate school. There are many nontraditional outlets that can be educational. One of my favorites is Coursera. You can take a university online class on nearly any subject. These classes are great refresher or introductory tool. Another unconventional resource is YouTube. Yes, THAT YouTube! It may come as a surprise to you but YouTube is not just videos of cats, funny children or horribly, hilarious falls. It also houses an infinite number of tutorials, workshop clips and online training videos. The last one I will recommend is the one I use the most: iTunes U. It is the world's largest catalog of free education content. There are over 750,000 free lectures, videos, books and other resources. With these devices at your disposal you are left without excuse!

As much as I love independent learning through modern systems, one can not become well-rounded when relying solely on online and/or distance learning. Several years ago I was having a conversations with a few acquaintances about mentoring. I was sharing a recent conversation I had with one of my mentors. My excitement was bubbling over and I found myself eager to share my newly gained knowledge with others. I asked the group if they had mentors and to my surprise nearly everyone said no. The most shocking thing of it all was that some looked at me like I was an alien because I had one. (I would rather not imagine the looks if they knew I have several! Yikes!!)

I was intrigued by that moment and set out on a quest to find out if this was a common theme, particularly with millennials. Disturbingly enough, it was! It wasn't just an issue with young adult, it was consistent among adults of all ages. I discovered that once they reach adulthood, many adults see mentoring strictly as something they do instead of something they receive.

"Fools are headstrong and do what they like; wise people take advice." Proverbs 12:15, MSG

Before we go into how you should acquire a mentor, let's solidify the meaning. One of the many definitions of mentor is "an experienced and trusted adviser." Your mentor is not the person who buys you nice gifts and takes you to fancy restaurants. While those blessings may come with the relationship, it is not the core of the interaction. Do NOT approach someone to be your mentor with hopes of what they can buy for you. Material gain should be the furthest thought from your mind. The Message Bible translation of Proverbs 27:17 says,

"You can use steel to sharpen steel, and one friend sharpens another."

Your only want in any mentor relationship should be growth. Your desire to simply become a better person will make you more teachable and open opportunities you never could have imagined. Humility opens doors that intelligence can't open.

Your mentor also does not have to be someone who lives in the same city. Technology has made the world seem so small. Make the most of social media, email, video chat and conference calls when it comes to connecting with a mentor. Remember, their wisdom and guidance is what you are seeking as opposed to their physical presence. Words know no distance.

I'm sure you are probably wondering where you should begin in that continuing education process and how you should find a mentor. Let's begin with the first portion. Every industry has its respective professional organizations. Wedding planners, caterers, motivational speakers, athletes. There is an organization to support you. If you cannot name that organization off the top of your head, stop right now and locate it. Professional organizations are also a great place to find a mentor. Make it your mission to attend their local, regional or national meetings. Attend their educational workshops and conferences. Set an educational goal for each quarter of the year.

The following five keys are sure to help you begin your mentor search.

1. Identify your goals

"And then God answered: "Write this. Write what you see. Write it out in big block letters so that it can be read on the run. This vision-message is a witness pointing to what's coming. It aches for the coming - it can hardly wait! And it doesn't lie. If it seems slow in coming, wait. It's on the way. It will come right on time." Habakkuk 2:2, MSG

You must know your intended destination before you seek help or guidance. Spend some alone time meditating and clearly understand what God has assigned you to do. Trust me, He will answer you. Sometimes we continue to question God and wait for answers to our follow up questions when He has already given a response. Begin to create with the pieces He has given you and watch Him put the puzzle together as you move. Solidify your goals by quarter, year, etc. It is essential to know where you desire to go prior to seeking advice from others. Without clear direction you may find yourself unintentionally swayed by the words of a mentor and following their goals instead of your own. Your mentor's advice is important but your mentor is not your god. Assignment comes from God.

2. Research your industry to find innovators

"God created human beings; He created them godlike, reflecting God's nature. He

created them male and female. He blessed them."
Genesis 1:27, MSG

God is the ultimate innovator! While our gifts and abilities are amazing they can not compete with creating the universe and all living creatures in merely six days. Be confident in what God has given you but trust what He has given to others as well. Do not be so arrogant to think you are the only trendsetter in your field. I have always admire the genius of the late, great Steve Jobs. His ability to think well beyond his current worldview sealed his fate as one of this generations greatest innovators. Anyone who aspires to be in the technology field should be familiar with him and Apple. I know some of you may think, "My business is unique. No one does what I do or want to do." Trust me, there is SOMEONE who can identify with your career path. They do not have to mirror your exact assignment but find someone who can relate. Find out who the leaders are in your city, region and globally.

3. Contact them

"Don't bargain with God. Be direct. Ask for what you need. This isn't a cat-and-mouse, hide-and-seek game we're in."
Matthew 7:7, MSG

I love the way The Message Bible puts that scripture. Just as we should be direct in our communication with God, this is the most important step in the process to finding a mentor. It is a simple act but can be the most intimidating one. Send a thoughtful email. Tweet them. Be honest but not creepy. Think of how you would want to be approached in a similar circumstance. Be respectful but go for it! Maintain that respect even if you are rejected. There is someone out there who will answer the call. It is up to you to find them! Seek God's counsel as you reach out to them.

4. Throw away your feelings

"No discipline seems pleasant at the time, but painful. Later on, however, it produces a harvest of righteousness and peace for those who have been trained by it."
Hebrew 12:11, NIV

A good mentor will not only build you up but tear you down when necessary. Embrace their criticism. They are speaking from a place of experience and have your best interest in mind. Do not wear your heart on your sleeve. This is not the time for sensitivity. The birthing process is not an easy one. It is painful and exhausting but that short time of discomfort does not compete with the joys of parenthood once the child arrives. The right mentor will come with an incredible amount of balance as it relates to correction. They understand the need for you to receive proper guidance but give it with love.

5. Repeat the process

"Without good direction, people lose their way; the more wise counsel you follow, the better your chances."
Proverbs 11:12, MSG

It is perfectly acceptable (and encouraged) to have more than one mentor. This will allow you to have multiple perspectives on a situation and diverse advice. More than likely your mentor will be someone who has a very demanding schedule. If you have more than one mentor, you are less likely to find yourself in a situation where you are in need of guidance and unable to reach your sensei.

After you have developed a relationship with your mentor be sure to show your appreciation for what they are sowing into your life. Be sure that you invest in their products when the opportunity avails. Support their business or speaking engagements. Lend your services to assist them in completing a project. Do not simply sit at the table just to eat. They worked hard to attain the intellect they have. Be respectful and show your gratefulness for their willingness to share their world with you.

There is no need to take this journey called life alone! Everyone needs a few people they can trust with lending words of wisdom in a serious situations. Get a mentor today. We all need one!

Chapter Two

"Remember: A stingy planter gets a stingy crop; a lavish planter gets a lavish crop." 2 Corinthians 9: 6, MSG

I love that scripture! It painted such a vivid picture in my head the minute I read it. Imagine this! You are best friends with a farmer. For the sake of this story let's call him John. You have known John since you were friends. He was raised in a family of farmers and has become very familiar with the industry. Every spring you know John is going to plant his crops and harvest them in the fall. You have started to look forward to both seasons for different reasons but the fall is your favorite. The excitement and pleasure John gets when harvesting his crops is incomparable. Planting and harvesting is not the only time John works. He is most dedicated and committed between those two segment of time. He knows (and you have come to know as well) that healthy crops will not grow if they are not properly maintained. One year John comes to you and tell you about a new crop he wants to harvest. You ask him when he plans to plant the seeds, how long it will take to harvest and all of the other questions you can think of. You are just as excited as he is about this new crop. His response startles you. "Oh, I'm not going to plant any seeds for this crop. I'm an experienced farmer. I grew up in a farming household and every year my crops are plentiful. I'm just going to pray and believe that God is going to allow me to reap this harvest." As a good friend it is your responsibility to tell John how much his idea is not a good one. I'm going to pause right now and address the naysayers who may say "John is just speaking in faith." In this story, that is not the case. God did not instruct John to do NOTHING and expect to receive a harvest. He is not making a faith move. He is refusing to put any work into a goal and expects his desires, reputation, familial history and previous success to be enough for future success. Now let's go back to what you would say to him. Would you encourage him to put in the work required to yield the harvest or would you join him in expectation of this unmerited harvest?

Hopefully by this point you have grasped the concept that your dream WILL require you to spend money. You invest in what you believe in! The same way we save to afford a luxury vacation, purchase a new home or even go out of our way to shop at our favorite stores is the same principle we should apply when it comes to investing into our businesses. Think about the last time you wanted to do or buy something in your personal life that you could not immediately afford. Go ahead, get that thought in your mind. I will wait for you. Got it? Great! What did you do so that you could make that "thing" happen? Did you reduce your number of shopping sprees? Eliminate items within your budget? How did it feel once you were able to do what you planned and saved to do? I'm sure you are probably starting to smile right now. That sense of accomplishment for a task that did not seem immediately accessible is like none other. Yes, you may have to push your target date back a few months until you have the funds readily available. Spend that time preparing to be sure that you are ready when it is time to push that big red button. (Not the easy button. That one does not work most of the time. Trust me!)

One of the most frustrating encounters I have as a marketing expert is when I meet an entrepreneur who wants the world but does not want to spend a dime to gain it. I am sure all of my fellow PR pros can understand that sentiment. About three years ago I met with a small business owner who wanted to grow their business. They had a nice product had great potential for success. They catered to the health conscious customer and the timing was perfect for them. The healthy food and exercise industries were seeing large growth as people became more engaged with living and maintaining healthier lifestyles. I was excited to hear their business plan and short-term goals. The most shocking moment of our meeting came when they said this to me, "Ty, we love what you do. We believe in our product and know you will help us make more money but we aren't able to spend anything at this time." Think about that statement for a moment. What would you think about an entrepreneur who approached you with the desire to work together but they have no desire to "put their money where their mouth is?" I'm sure your thoughts are less than favorable. Mind you, I did not have a previous relationship with this potential client. To them, I was the public relations expert they found on the internet. So let's think about this again. They had a great product, incomplete business plan and a need for marketing services but no motive to put in the required investment. Doesn't that remind you of John? I know the story seems a bit extreme but it is very practical. It is irrational to expect to receive when you have not given anything. Passion alone is not enough. It is necessary but it cannot be the only way you expect to survive.

If you do not believe in your brand enough to invest your money in it, why should a venture capitalist or customer give you their hard earned money? You must be the first partaker. I know. I can hear you saying it now, "But Ty I don't have the money and that's why I need investors." You will have to make sacrifices, cut costs and eliminate unnecessary expenses. Trim the fat. Get on a strict budget. Reduce your production costs even if that means switching to a new vendor. It becomes easier to walk away from something when you have no invested value in it. Your time and energy are investments but so is your money. If you want it bad enough you will find a way. Do not let the lack of money be your excuse to remain stagnant or below average. Cash is plentiful and can be easily obtained. The key is knowing where to look to make and save more of it.

Now that we are on the same page about whether or not you will have to spend money. Let's talk about a few areas where you can expect to spend money when it comes to creating or rebuilding a brand. The logo is the first item that presents a company to the public so we will begin there. Before we go into the details of a logo I want to be sure we are on the same page about what a logo is and is not. It is defined as "a distinctive company signature, trademark, etc." Distinctive is the key word in that phrase. Taking a picture you found online and placing your company's name over it is not a logo. That is actually a dangerous practice that could cause you to be in violation of someone's copyright protection. You need permission to use any photos you find online. Just because you located it via the Google Images search tool does not mean it is license free. I will not go into the details of creative commons but it is something every innovator should be familiar with.

Even if you are not a fan of fast food I am sure you have never mistaken a Wendy's sign for a McDonald's sign. The logos are very unique and are a clear representation of their corresponding brands. A good logo is distinct enough to be noticed but simplistic enough to be understood. Coca-Cola, Apple, Starbucks, Nike and Lexus. Every one of those logos are easy to recognize. They are simple, clean and clear. The logo is not the place to incorporate 20 different symbols that have meaning to you. It is not your chance to tell a complex story with words. Do not misunderstand what I am saying. Your logo can have a deeper meaning but it should be done in simplistic fashion. What do I mean by this? Apple is a great example. Their logo is a simple apple with a bite taken out of it. The meaning behind it has a biblical reference. Genesis talks about Adam and Eve taking a bite out of fruit from the tree of knowledge of good and evil. Apple's founders had the goal of exposing people to a newer level of thought, consciousness and intelligence through their products. While the fruit seems fitting to represent a company of the same name, it has a more involved meaning than what meets the eye. Steve Jobs and Steve Wozniack came up with and agreed on how the logo would look but I can assure you they did not design it themselves. They were not graphic artists so they yielded to the expertise of someone else.

This is one area you will have to invest in but you will not regret it. An experienced and talented graphic artist will have the ability to bring your words to life. You may use a sketch pad or a word document to come up with the inspiration for your logo but it should not be where your design is finalized. A graphic artist will take your design to the next level and give you first class imagery with the ability to compete with Fortune 500 companies. They will also understand the importance of having a simple, clean and clear image to serve as your insignia. You should also be sure that you pay a little extra to have it converted into multiple file types and receive the original layered file. If none of what I said makes sense to you, have no fear. Just tell your graphic desires your requests and they will know exactly what you mean. I promise! If they don't, they are not as experienced as they have represented and may not be the graphic designer for you. Spend your money and your time wisely.

Your logo will follow your company for a long time. It should not be changed every quarter or every year. When you constantly change your brand's imagery it ruins the validity of it. Do not mistake this to mean you cannot refresh your brand or improve when necessary. The entire premise of this book is based on creating and recreating a brand. You CAN make brand changes. If you know it is broken, please fix it. However, you should not find yourself with a new logo every season or every year. Think about the brands we discussed earlier in this chapter. When is the last time any of them changed their logo? I am sure you can think of a recent, major change for every one of them. The reason it is so recognizable is because they understand the power of consistency. Coca-Cola has had nearly twenty logos in its 128 year history. Yes, twenty. I encourage you to research them right now. While they have made slight changes to it every few years it did not change drastically. A few of the logos are so similar that you may feel as if you are playing a game while trying to find the differences between them. They understand the power that this graphic holds and drastic changes to it will have adverse effects. The last thing you want to do is get your audience used to your logo then start the process all over again because of a change. If you are not rebuilding your brand as a whole, be careful with changing your logo.

The next thing I want us to examine is your website. Do you have one? If your do, what is the web address? Say it aloud. Right now. If you said anything that includes the name of a company besides yours (.wordpress .wix .weebly, etc.) then this portion is just for you. Nascar is a very engaging sport. Some of you may think it is the high speed or rivalries that I consider engaging. Not at all! I am always interested to see what companies have sponsored drivers. I am not a Nascar follower so outside of the Earnhardt men, Danicka Patrick and Mario Andretti, I don't know many names. That in mind, I don't think of many other drivers when I see the cars. I see their sponsors. I watch and cheer based on the sponsoring companies. Even when the race is over the drivers are wearing gear with the companies' logos. As someone who is not familiar with their individual careers, I associate them with what I see. Keep that in mind with your website. If your business card says "mybusiness.someonelsesbiz.com" then you are doing the same thing a Nascar driver does. They are professionals who are paid to represent their other brands. Are you freely allowing another company to advertise themselves in the space that is reserved for you?

I am stepping on some toes but I want the best for you. Remember, we put our feelings away during mentoring moments. *smile* It is not the end of the world if your website is guilty of free advertisement in the web address. You have the ability to purchase your domain at any time. Your web host can assist you with this process. If you do not see it by logging in to your account, contact customer support and let them know you want to buy your domain. Put this on the top of your to-do list. It is essential that you are the only brand represented in your web address. You have earned that spot.

Before you hang up with your web host, purchase an email plan as well. Gmail is my preferred personal email service. I love their calendar integration, Google Voice and other services. That is not the email I give for business. The email I give is ty@elevatyd.com. Makes sense, right? I have a full email plan for my team and our associated projects. There is a major difference between John@Farmville.com and JohnFarmville@gmail.com. The former is solely about John of Farmville. That is how it should be. The latter is about John of Farmville and Google's email service. Are you thinking about our Nascar conversation again? They are very similar.

Your web address should also be something that is easy to understand, correlate and remember. If you operate Larry's Lawn Service then I can understand if your website is larryslawn.com or larryslawnservice.com. I can even understand yourlawnservice.com or bestlawnservice.com. The same simple, clean and clear focus we take when creating a logo is the same focus that is necessary when creating a website. This goes for the design as well. I implore you to seek the assistance of web developer. If you are in the beginning stages and do not have the funds to spend on an advanced website, there are other resources. Fiverr.com is one of my favorites when it comes to completing tasks with a small budget. You can find just about ANYTHING on this site. It is not the same as working with a web builder you can call, text or email at any time but it is the best alternative I had found to date. Start there. The inability to build an advanced website with the best graphics is not an acceptable reason to have a subpar website.

We have a great logo, professional email and our perfect domain. What do you think is next? If you guess business cards then you deserve a gold star. Pull out your business card and examine everything on the front and back of it. Your logo is clean. Your website is memorable. Your email is professional... but the card is bent, a stain is on the front, there is random writing on your card where you tested a pen and the back says "printed by _____." I understand if you printed your first batch through a service that offer free production because that is what you could afford at the time. If you take nothing else from this book pay attention to this part. After you have purchased your domain (for less than the price of lunch) purchase a new set of business cards that do not advertise another business (for less than the price of a full tank of gas.) Yes, you can get your domain and high quality business cards for those estimations.

Since we have tapped into print jobs, let's tackle flyers, brochures and other print collateral. I need you to use your imagination again for this story. Your are a new to a city and are looking for a local bakery. You are hosting a housewarming party and would like an assortment of desserts for your guests. Baking isn't your strong suit so you decide to pick up a few treats. (Bakers, I said use your imagination. I heard your "Oh no, I can bake" response.) You ask a colleague for a recommendation and they suggest a popular bakery downtown. As you are out running errands, you search for the bakery online so you can use GPS but are unable to find an address or phone number. (We will deal with that one later.) You brush it off and call your colleague and they give you exact directions to the business. When you arrive, you look for the name but there is no sign outside. You know you are in the correct place because you were told it was a pink building. You side eye the lack of street signs, business hours or any other signage on the outside of the building. You enter and an extremely polite employee greets you. She asks if you know what you would like or if you need a few minutes. You explain that it may take a little while to narrow the choices. Before you know it the two of you are engaged in a conversation about your recent move, pending housewarming and customers' favorite treats. You find yourself so pleased by her product knowledge and exceptional customer service. She hands you a menu and your joy is deflated like a popped balloon. It is a photocopy of a nicely produced menu. It's clear the original was in color because some portions of this black and white copy in your hand are illegible. It was copied at any angle so some of the words are cut off on the page. The opposite side has the old phone number scratched out in pen and the new one written above it. You decide you should stop looking and focus on the food. The employee asks if you would like a sample of anything and you oblige, albeit totally nervous. After one bite of the petit four you feel like you have just taken off in a hot air balloon. The taste is immaculate! You are immediately confused. How is it that a business this wonderful with extraordinary employees and tasty treats could be so haphazard when it comes to their brand? You notice the establishment is spotless but the menu is trashy. Why?

I have discovered that usually people take cheaper routes because they assume that is takes an astronomical amount of money to purchase a domain, setup email and print quality graphics. The fear of the unknown immobilizes them and they make an uninformed decision in haste. Allow me to deal with fear and intimidation for a moment.

"Don't fret or worry. Instead of worrying, pray. Let petitions and praises shape your worries into prayers, letting God know your concerns. Before you know it, a sense of God's wholeness, everything coming together for good, will come and settle you down. It's wonderful what happens when Christ displaces worry at the center of your life." Philippians 4:6-7, MSG

I. Love. The. Message. Bible!!! It makes the scriptures so real and personal. That last sentence excited me! "It's wonderful what happens when Christ displaces worry at the center of your life." I know we are discussing branding but I already told you that God is the ultimate brand maker and innovator. He is always appropriate in our conversation. Instead of making a decision that you have not researched, are unsure about or just want to do it to get it done, PRAY. I know that seems so simple and obvious to say but it's necessary. Remove the worry and allow Christ to rest in the place where worry once resided. Imagine what would happen if the time we spent worrying was spent meditating on the beautiful things of God. The next two verses of the same passage are even more exhilarating.

"Summing it all up, friends, I'd say you'll do best by filling your minds and meditating on things true, noble, reputable, authentic, compelling, gracious - the best, not the worst; the beautiful, not the ugly; things to praise, not things to curse. Put into practice what you learned from me, what you heard and saw and realized. Do that and God, who makes everything work together, will work you into his most excellent harmonies." Philippians 4:8-9. MSG

Take a praise break. I encourage it.

SECTION TWO

An overnight success is actually the result of several long nights!

Chapter Three

I want us to examine the philosophies Ray Kroc and S. Truett Cathy for a moment. For those who recognize those names you are probably what those two have in common. How is it possible that the men behind the machines we have come to know as McDonald's and Chik-fil-A can be easily compared? I assure you this stretches beyond both of them being fast food restaurants. In 1954 Ray Kroc was a vendor for McDonald's, distributing multi-mixers to then owners Richard and Maurice McDonald. He became intrigued by the restaurant when he noticed their orders for his product were very large. The business was small but effective. Their menu of simply burgers, fries and drinks allowed them to focus on the details of each item. This was their key to success in consistently producing a high quality product. One year later Kroc fully developed a partnership with the brothers and founded the McDonald's corporation. His goal was to replicate the process he saw in San Bernandino, California in restaurants all over the world by franchising the brand. Kroc wanted the customers to receive the same taste, service and experience in every McDonald's no matter the location. The primary goal was to build a template that would not only become familiar with the employees but also the customers. A resident of New York could dine at a restaurant in New Mexico and have the confidence of encountering friendly faces while ordering their favorite meal. Ray Kroc created the signature experience and made it one other entrepreneurs wanted to take part in. He coined the phrase, "In business for yourself but not by yourself." The idea was that with a partnership between the McDonald's corporation, a supplier and a franchisee, each would mutually benefit from the relationship. The franchisees were treated as partners in an environment where innovation was encourage and responsibility was taken. This approach yielded some of the restaurants most famous items including the Big Mac, Filet-O-Fish and Egg McMuffin. The golden arches can now be seen all across the globe. He knew the value of being a recognizable and reliable brand even when it was just a small restaurant in California.

Chicken sandwich, waffle fries and closed on Sundays. That's right! I'm thinking about S. Truett Cathy's Chik-fil-A. 1946 brought the birth of The Dwarf Grill, which would later spawn the creation of the popular restaurant. Cathy and his brother, Ben, made $58.20 in sales during their first day of operation. Pause and let that sink in for a second. The fast food restaurant that is currently the most profitable per store (earning nearly $3 million per location) made less than sixty dollars in its first day.

"Even the largest avalanche is triggered by small things." -Vernor Vinge

It is often difficult to continue through the down or disappointing times in a business. Do not let those moments overtake your memories, make you miserable and become your life.

Truett Cathy operated according to his Five-Step Recipe for Business Success. One of those tenets is to create a loyalty effect. In his book, *Eat Mor Chikin: Inspire More People,* Cathy states, "The bottom line is that our people, from our restaurant Operators to the team members they hire, enjoy their work. Fewer than five percent of our franchise Operators leave the chain in any given year. The more we can foster the feeling that we are a group of people working together, depending on each other, the more likely we are to be loyal to each other." Cathy was committed to growing his business from the inside out. Like Kroc, he understood the importance of selling your ideology to your team and empowering them to be a face of the brand. I have seen many business owners and leaders wonder why they are struggling with their sales or growth. They have a great product, are familiar with their target market, strategic campaigns but they do not see improvements or even face decline. It is impossible to grow your business if it does not build a reputation of reliability. That construct begins internally with your employees or leadership then extends outwardly to your customer, client or member. Truett Cathy knew the value of being a reliable brand long before they became the nation's largest quick-service chicken restaurant.

Ray Kroc and Truett Cathy knew the type of companies they wanted to create before they existed. They saw the vision before it materialized. It was easy for them to construct a signature look that stood out amongst their competition but it was not a haphazard act. Ray Kroc saw McDonald's as an international brand when they were a neighborhood barbecue restaurant. Truett Cathy envisioned a chorus of followers singing the praises of Chik-fil-A even when they made less than sixty dollars on their first day. It was easy for them to be confident in their approach and to build a distinguishable identity because they were clear about it from the beginning.

Can you say the same? One of the most important things to remember, as you make your journey through entrepreneurship or even leadership, is your identity. Never forget the reason you started the business. Remind yourself of your ultimate goal. Keep in mind the environment you wanted to foster amongst your employees and customers. Remind yourself what you want your customers to experience. I know it may seem like an overwhelming idea at times especially when you are between two seasons. You know the place between "I'm not struggling as much as I used to" and "I can charter a jet overseas." Does that sound familiar to you? It is easy for frustration to set in during those moments but I am here to help you redirect your energy.

"If people can't see what God is doing, they stumble all over themselves; But when they attend to what he revels, they are most blessed." Proverbs 29:18, MSG

That scripture is so simple but so profound. In my early years, like many entrepreneurs, I found myself obsessing over every detail. I would get so caught up in trying to make everything perfect that I would become stuck in incompletion. I misunderstood the wisdom of being prepared and having my ducks in a row. I thought that meant that I needed to have every aspect perfect before I could do anything. The things I could not figure out or did not know made me anxious. I prayed to God so passionately one day until I was soaked with tears. I cried myself to sleep and had one of the most vivid dreams I ever had! In the dream God told me to work what He gave me to the best of my ability. He reminded me of my identity and what sets me apart from others. I woke up energized and full of creativity. I started to write down my plans and turn my attention to developing my signature. Each day I reviewed it until it became something I knew without needing notes. I placed notes in my car, my bedroom, my bathroom and set several reminders in our phone. I knew I had to sell the vision to myself because I could sell it to anyone else. As I worked the elements that I was familiar with, the others began to come together. Throughout the development stages, I never lost track of what makes me recognizable.

It is easy to get distracted by what you do not know or what is not working. Let's not get confused. I'm not saying that research is not required and passion alone is enough. I'm also not saying that you shouldn't take notes from your failures and learn from them. My advice here is direct.

Do not become so exhausted by the idea of the journey that you never take the first step. We get so overwhelmed by totality of a task that we never begin. Don't let fear cripple you. Remind yourself of what you know. Grow your confidence in that and build your foundation. Become so comfortable with your reason for being, your purpose and your goal that even in the toughest, saddest and most disappointing moments you are able to fight your way back to the pursuit of greatness.

Having and perfecting an elevator pitch is a great way to affirm yourself. (It is also an essential to success. EVERYONE needs one.) Think about this. You stop by the grocery store on the way home from work. It's a been a long week and you are completely exhausted. You are wearing a polo shirt with your company's logo on it. The person standing next to you inquires about your business. Your energy level is on level two on a scale of one to ten but you hear your mentor's voice in your head. "Make sure you are always ready to pitch at any moment." You strike up a conversation with the customer and you learn they are a senior executive at a company you have been researching for months. You have been preparing and deciding on your method of approach so you may pitch your company's services to them and here you are having small talk with their senior vice president. At the end of the conversation the two of you have exchanged contact information and scheduled a lunch meeting for the following week.

Sounds like a very inspirational encounter, right? I agree! I felt the same way when my client recounted her story to me. Yes, that's a true story. My client was moved to tears. "I remembered all the times you made me give you my elevator pitch over and over. Honestly, sometimes I sounded like a broken record but in that moment your purpose was very clear to me. I had no issues telling him about my services and products. My confidence went through the roof as we spoke. I answered his questions quickly and concisely. You always tell me to prepare for tomorrow and I'm so grateful I was ready."

Preparation is the bridge between your dream and your reality. It does not matter what your aspirations are if you are not ready when the opportunity presents itself. Yes. I understand that you will never know when that chance may happen. The best way to be sure you don't miss the moment that is destined for you is to be prepared at all times. What's your elevator pitch? If I asked you to tell me what you do, the services you provide and/or your product, what would you say? We are going to review the fundamentals of an elevator pitch.

Name

I know it seems very simple but I cannot tell you how many times I have heard a pitch that did not include the person or company's name. Your name should be the first thing that is said.

This would also be a good place to insert your personal mantra or business motto.

Description

This part may take a little time to perfect. You want to be clear but also succinct. This is not the time to give a rundown of every previous client, service project or business experience. Decide on the portion of your business that you want to highlight the most. It may be different depending on your setting, audience or what you are currently trying to promote so it is wise to make sure you have a few options to choose from.

Market

As a business professional you easily be able to identify the problem that you solve in the world through your product or service. Understanding the problem you solve will help you figure out the audience you reach. We will talk about target market a little later so there is no need to worry if you are unsure about what you should say in this section.

Similarities

Yes, there is a business or product that is similar to yours. Notice I did not say identical. When you explain your similarities that gives the person you are speaking to a foundation to build upon in the conversation. This will also keep you from running in circles or being very wordy when attempting to explain yourself.

Differences

I'm pretty sure some of you are letting out a sigh of relief. If you turned your nose up at mentioning a similar company, trust me it is with good reason. This is where you shine. Here is the occasion to differentiate your brand from everyone else's. Standing out in the crowd does not mean that you have to bash the next person or business. Do not EVER use this or any other platform as your invitation to speak negatively about someone else.

Goals

Remember the problem you are called to solve? This is valuable to this section as well. Summarize what you do, who you serve and your ultimate goal. It may take some time to perfect this to the ideal length. Keep working at it until it sounds like music to your ears.

Take a look at this example of an elevator pitch using the model above:

"My name is Jane Doe and I am the founder of Creative Design Solutions. We are a full service graphic design and print company. We are located in the New Orleans area but we also ship to clients located throughout the United States. Our structure is similar to FedEx Office but we specialize in creating design options for our customers to choose from. We have the ability to print ready-made projects but we also develop original designs. We aim to become the leading collateral and imaging solution for small businesses fulfilling every need from business cards to building signage to tradeshow displays."

You have a pretty good idea of what Creative Design Solutions does and it didn't take thirty minutes to get to that point. While the pitch followed the structure it did not seem forced or disjointed. Pause right now and develop or refine your elevator pitch. Practice it in the mirror, in front of your friends and with your team. Everyone on your staff should be able give an elevator pitch as well.

There's no need to become frustrated or discouraged if you don't get it right the first time. Building a recognizable brand is a consistent process. You will always have and need an elevator pitch. Take your time with the development but work diligently.

Chapter Four

Your branding efforts can only be as successful as they are thorough. Attention to every detail is essential. Many entrepreneurs and executives would like to think they market to everyone. Some would probably say they market to teens, moms or small business owners. Those categories are far too large for an effective marketing campaign. Moms and preteens do not share the same values, concerns or priorities. I am sure every parent can agree with that statement. Tide finds little to no value in advertising to preteens. Most children are not responsible for their own laundry and they do not make buying decisions for the household. Conversely, Lucky Charms and other similar cereals will spend more of their marketing dollars on communicating with children. While it is still true that children do not make the buy decisions, this is definitely a situation where they would influence the choices of the parent by expressing their preferences. Therefore, it becomes challenging to run a campaign for a product where you are trying to connect with so many types of people at the same time. Let me pause right here and give some clarity. I am not saying the product CANNOT be marketed to many audiences. I am saying it would take a different campaign for each one. If you take nothing else from this book please understand how essential it is to get to know your potential customer as much as possible prior to asking them for anything. The depth of your prior research will be evident through your campaign's effectiveness.

The best place to begin any marketing or brand development strategy is research. I know you are probably wondering exactly what you are supposed to research. I have outline the early steps for you. Let's take a look at each area.

Current Customer

If you are still in the early stages of development this part may not be as relative to you right now. Take note of it and remember it for the near future. Whether you have been established for one month or one decade you should have demographics for your current customers. This is another area where "EVERYONE" is the wrong answer. While you may desire to work with everyone or your current range may seem extremely broad, there needs to be more definition to your customer's identity. Your entire team should know without a doubt what makes them different from the competitor. If they are unable to clearly express this to a potential customer or partner, it is not their fault. As the leader your responsibility is to make sure that everyone is on the same page and well trained. Some professionals miss this part. They train their employees on the systems and products they carry but they do not discuss their competitors. This is critical. Who currently uses your product? Where do they live? Age? Gender?

Here's one way to figure this out. Create a spreadsheet focused strictly on customer demographics and update it on at least a weekly or biweekly basis. If you provide a service where you have the ability to see your clientele or have information profiles on hand, begin to make note of every detail you can about your consumer. Start with the following categories: age, location, gender, ethnicity, how did they hear about you. You can add more as you go along. If you do not have the ability to see your customers in person then begin to send surveys to your email database. Request similar information about them. Note: Some people may not be comfortable answering some of the listed questions. I encourage you to make the response fields optional. You don't want to turn your customer into a detractor because they were offended by your persistence in knowing their age, race or gender.

When creating your spreadsheet, include a separate sheet for social media interaction and content about new and returning customers. This will be useful for discovering your customer acquisition and retention rates, even if you are not engaging in social media ad buys. The online engagement will give you an idea of the customers who may interested but have not been converted to purchasers. Use this data to discover more about their behaviors so you may adequately advertise to them and turn them into buyers. It is rude to ask someone to buy into your product or service and you have no idea who they are. Be kind and you will not only have a customer but a promoter.

Industry

This one seems so elementary that it is often overlooked. Most people start their businesses out of the desire to pursue a talent or solve a problem. They can spend so much time engrained in their product and business plan that they forget to consider the industry they are in. You are an aspiring filmmaker but you have no idea what programs are the industry's standard. Yes, you have a gift for creativity in film but would you be ready if MGM called you to partner with you? Are you current productions ready for the next level? I can hear some of you saying, "But Ty, that's just it! I was called to change the standards in my industry." That may be the case but consider Proverbs 19:2, NIV. "Desire without knowledge is not good -- how much more will hasty feet miss the way." The Message Bible is very straightforward with it. "Ignorant zeal is worthless; haste makes waste." Be sure that you are knowledgeable of the climate and consistencies in your industry prior to making strides to completely going against the grain.

Competition

If you responded to this question by saying, "I don't have competition. I'm in a lane of my own." I must disagree with you. Even the most creative inventions have competition. Candles were the competition for light bulbs. Horse drawn carriages were the competition for cars. Typewriters were the competition to computers. Do you get my drift? You have not done enough research if you think nothing or no one is currently in your lane. Either a similar product or service currently exists or the problem you are looking to solve is being solved by other means. What I mean by that is there is another way to handle the issue. Consider this. In 2013 I was watching one of my favorite shows, *Shark Tank*, and the product Spatty Daddy was being featured. I'm going to pause right here and implore you to watch *Shark Tank* if you aren't already a fan. Entrepreneurs bring their products and/or business to millionaires in hopes of partnering with them to grow their businesses. Their pitch must be just as on point as their invention or company. Mark Cuban and Daymond John are two of the most notable sharks, who are also potential investors. Trust me. You will be inspired and intrigued by this show. Ok, back to Spatty Daddy. Imagine a tiny spatula with a long handle and you have the Spatty Daddy. During their pitch they mentioned that consumers waste nearly 25% of their product because so much of it is left behind in the bottle. Think of your bottle of lotion. No matter how long you let it sit upside down, there will be a great amount of the product that remains. Enter the Spatty! It is designed so you can get the maximum use out of your products. Sounds rather simple yet smart, right? Product waste is something everyone can relate to. It will vary how much each person cares about it but it still exists. The competition for Spatty Daddy is the trash. Everyone will not care enough about getting the last bit of lotion or shampoo to invest in the product. It may be more of a hassle than a convenience for others. Your customers always have the choice of doing nothing to solve their problem. This can be another issue of its own; however, it is still seen as competition. Always remember that your customer has options. What are they? What do they provide or do that you do not? Is that a good thing that your services are not the same? How will you educate them on the differences? In order for you to educate your customers, you have to become well versed in the subject matter. What would be the reasons a potential consumer would decline your service or product? Have you worked to understand why and how you can eliminate those reasons? This is your competition.

Study your competitors on every level. Find out who looks like you locally, regionally, nationally and internationally. Review their business model. Discover what has worked for them and what has not. This will not only enhance your business acumen but will also give you a blueprint. There is nothing wrong with being inspired by the work of others. I didn't want to give this disclaimer but I felt it was necessary for clarity. Understand me clearly when I say I am not encouraging plagiarism, copyright infringement or anything else that violates someone's creative rights. It is NEVER appropriate to take credit for someone else's work. It is never acceptable. The benefit of researching someone else's work is to learn from their mistakes. Many entrepreneurs has made good and bad decisions. Every successful entrepreneur has failed at least once. They became successful by weeding out the wrong ways to get the finish line. Learn as much as you can from others. (Sounds like the mentoring segment, right? I know.)

Unique

This area is probably much easier to tackle. Think of EVERYTHING that makes you different from your competition. (See how important it is to learn about your competition?) We talked about this briefly with the elevator pitch but let's go into it a bit more. What would make someone leave the comfort of their current resource, product or service and move to new and unknown territory with you? Put your mind in that of a customer for this one. It can be a challenge for creators to think on the level of a consumer but it is essential at all times. Have you ever asked someone what made their business different and the answer confused you? They said something that was not a unique quality because you could immediately think of more than one business who did the same thing. Upon further questioning you realized that they had not investigated this area much, if at all. Do not be salon owner who says, "My business is different because my clients can schedule appointments online and we offer refreshments while they are being serviced." The list of salons like this is pretty long in my area. In a smaller city or rural area this may be an unprecedented feature. This is where research comes in handy. You don't want to open a restaurant and use the tagline "The only restaurant in the city offering all organic ingredients." Have you research other healthy restaurants to see if their ingredients are organic? It may not be in their slogan or advertised heavily but know these things before you make your claim. If you find you are the only, or the first then by all means, use that to your advantage. Just be sure your declaration of distinction truly exists. You will damage your credibility if your customers find out your word cannot be trusted.

No matter the status or success you and your business attain, seek to remain relatable to your audience. When your audience disconnects from you, they no longer care what makes you unique. They will forget why they choose to fight with parking hassles at your location, drive 20 minutes out of the way or pay more for your product. Maintain your focus on what sets you apart and makes you great. Maintain your connection with the people. Sometimes your customer can tell you what makes you unique better than you can. They have experienced your competitors and they are familiar with other ways of solving their problem. This is where a focus group is required. Most larger corporations have a very structured way of developing a focus group. Entrepreneurs and small business owners, if you do not have a focus group. Create one! Grab your most trusted colleagues, mentors and loved ones for this task. It is essential to effective growth.

Internal

Now that you have defined your ideal customer and understand what your competition is up to, are you prepared for the battle of the market? Is your website user friendly? Do you have a social media presence where your customers exist? Does your brand imaging need an overhaul? Is your logo a great representation of your company? Are your employees professional and exemplify your company's mission statement? Is your office/store clean and inviting to clients? I know this section is full of questions but I really want you to think about every aspect of your business from employees to business cards and flyers to building to digital presence. Are you equipped to win customers and lifetime promoters of your business? Here is an exercise that I want everyone to do. You will participate and I want you to choose at least one other person to do it as well. Pick someone else who may not be as engulfed in your business as you are. It can be a colleague, family member or neighbor. Go through the steps below and both of you will take note of your experiences.

1. Visit the company's social media pages. Have they been updated recently? Do the posts make sense? Are they full of grammatical errors? Do they respond to the inquiries and comments posted? Are the graphics appealing?

2. Google the business' name. Are the responses related to the business? Do you see their website listed?

3. Visit the website. Is it user-friendly? Are you able to access it from your smartphone?

4. If applicable, visit the physical location. Are the outdoor signs clear and easy to read? Is exterior clean and appealing? Is the interior clean and appealing? Are the employees friendly and knowledgeable? Are they professional and easy to identify?

5. Rate your experience on a scale of 1 to 10, with 10 signifying an excellent encounter. Would you visit again? Would you recommend this business to your friends and family?

The responses you receive should let you know if your business needs a makeover. Every now and then it can be a challenge to pull your head out of your situation and see the truth for what it really is. Thorough research of your business and strategies should be a regular practice. Avoid getting so caught up in achieving the next thing that you have no idea what is currently happening. Another favorite show of mine is *Undercover Boss*. On this show, company executives go undercover as new employees in their own companies. They participate in various channels of the business so they can become familiar with the practice on the front line. This exercise teaches them what works, what has not worked and what needs to be changed. You may not have thousands of employees but take a few hours and work "in the trenches" with them to see if anything needs to be revised.

Potential customer

I purposely made the first and sections about customers. They are the lifeline of any business and should be considered in every decision. Describe your ideal and desired customers. Where do they work? Where do they shop? Where do they live? What are they currently using to manage the problem your business is solving? What methods of communication do they prefer? What or who influences their buying decision. Now, does your description of your ideal customer match the one of your current customer? No need to worry, the answer has been 'no' every time I have given this survey to clients. That is perfectly OK! This does not mean you are not happy with your current customers. Room for growth is always a good thing. Research everything you know about your ideal customer. This will help you understand how to communicate with them.

I hope you noticed the common theme of research in every key. It is the most vital part of any marketing campaign. This is just a portion of an effective marketing plan. Take your time with each section. Be efficient but thorough. If you skip over any sections you will find yourself exhausting unnecessary marketing funds.

SECTION THREE

Don't be so protective of your dream that you suffocate it!

Chapter Five

By this point you have probably figured out that I like to share stories when illustrating a point. Here's another one. This experience is courtesy of a young woman named Brooklyn. Brooklyn was getting ready to host her annual Christmas party. This was her fifth consecutive year and the expectation was high. Two days before the event she was doing her usual last minute preparations. Venue walkthrough? Check. Decorations? Check. Caterer? Check. Entertainment? Check. She was so thrilled with the progress and her guests were just as excited. She had the perfect gown and she decided to give it one last whirl in the mirror when the unthinkable happened. She tripped over the train of the dress, her heel got caught and it ripped an enormous hole into her perfect gown. Here she sat on the floor of her room with less than 48 hours until her favorite occasion of the year. Over 150 guest would be in attendance. Family members, colleagues and potential donors for her nonprofit would be in the building. Every element of the night was taken care of except for her dress. She called her sister who recommended she look on Instagram for a couple of local boutiques. With a list of recommendations, she began her search. The first boutique had a private account so she moved on to the next one. She was working against the clock and was too frustrated to hope her request to follow was approved in time. The second boutique had one picture posted, which was shared 48 weeks ago. She clicked on the website and was unable to access it. The dreaded "unable to access the page" message popped up. She closed the browser and went back to Instagram. She prayed the third time would be the charm and it was. This boutique had several photos of their products and she found a dress that she loved. She commented on the photo and inquired about ordering it. While she waited on a response from them, she went to Google and searched for the boutique to find a website or physical location. The results were nothing related to the boutique in her city so her anxiety began to return. She called her sister to ask if she knew of the location of the boutique but she didn't. She informed her they recently moved but she didn't know exactly where. She began to feel sad all over again so she just sat on her bed in tears.

Now, I know some people may not see that situation as a true crisis but let's look at it a bit deeper. Brooklyn is a very influential national leader. Her nonprofit work had granted her access to world leaders and celebrities alike. Through it all, she remained very grounded. She lived in the city she was raised and believed in supporting entrepreneurs. She did not wear major labels because she believed in investing in her community. Every time she was photographed wearing a budding designers clothing, that respective label gained major traction. She knew the impact it would have so she did not see an ordinary department store as an option. All three businesses failed at making sure they were accessible online. Let's take a look at each situation. I have seen each one of them in real life and trust me, it effects your bottom line. You never know who is trying to become your customer.

The first boutique had a private account. A business or public figure having a private social media account is an oxymoron. What are you "hiding" from other people? The products you want to sell? I am going to dispel a myth that has been spreading like wildfire. There is NO WAY to keep someone else from seeing your photos online. Once you share content over the web it is there forever. It may not show on your account but it CAN be found. Having a private online account is a false sense of security. What happens if someone you follows shares your images somewhere you don't want them to be seen? What do you do if a person who follows you is hacked? If you approve every follow request on Twitter and Instagram, what is the point of having a private account? There is no reason for a business to have a private account. I understand that you may not want your family photos and other content shared with the general public. Create a separate account and share your personal content there. Your business should have a Facebook page instead of a Facebook profile. The number of followers will be unlimited and the content shared from the page is accessible by the general public. This will allow you to keep your professional and personal information separate.

The second boutique is one of the most common online issues I see with brands. The Facebook, Instagram or Twitter account was setup but it has not been used or updated in nearly a year or more. The website was active at one point but it was never renewed. Now the domain has been released and people who are searching to do business with you think your business has closed. There is no benefit in creating account on every social media outlet if they will not be properly managed. Figure out the social media tools used most by your target audience and grow your following on those outlets. If you do not have the time to manage your accounts, assign a team member or hire a social media manager. The reality of the world we live in is that people judge you based on your online presence. This remain constant when it comes to business and professional images presence through a tweet, Facebook post or the infamous "this page is parked free" message. What will others see when they search for your business online? We will touch on this later but consider that for a moment.

The third boutique is also a normal occurrence for businesses that are experiencing growth at a rapid pace. The website and social media accounts are created and active but they are a little outdated. The new information has not been updated at this point and you feel no information is the best way to go. You post content about your products and/or services but you do not respond to any comments or requests. Your online presence is very one-dimensional and far from interactive. Why is this an issue, you ask? According to a recent *Forbes* study, 78% of consumers say a company's social media posts influence their buying decisions. Social media has become an essential extension of all marketing plans. In the past five years, social media outlets have been the key to success for so many breakout brands. YouTube gave us Justin Bieber. He began uploading videos to his YouTube channel in 2007. They eventually ended up in the hands of Usher, who became his mentor. Alex Tanney went undrafted after leaving Monmouth College. A video of him making trick throws gained traction the eventual attention of many NFL general managers. Tanney has since been on a few NFL teams, including being the backup quarterback for the Dallas Cowboys. That's right, all from YouTube. Google is no longer a noun but a verb, as well as a common practice for the average consumer. Want to see what movies are playing tonight? Google it. Taking a vacation and want to know the best hotels in the area? Google it. Want to try a new Italian restaurant? Google it. What happens when your brand's name is searched in Google?

If you aren't represented at the table, you can't be given a hand to play. Your first responsibility is to do all that you can to get to the table. Social media is no longer an optional means of communication for brands. Long gone are the days where Facebook was just for college students. Facebook and its billions of users have become a great resource for connecting with current and potential customers. Social media is a great tool to use to grow your brand. Refusing to capitalize on it to help improve your digital footprint is far from wise, especially if your marketing budget is low or close to nonexistent. Start where you are! Don't let it be the thing you buried in the ground. Use all that you have. Come to the table.

Make sure you are prepared when you come to the table. We have discussed the importance of investing in quality graphics. You are judged by your online appearance. Your consumer makes a judgment call about your brand based on what they see online. What would you think if Target's website was inactive? You would probably be shocked that the retail giant did not have a working website. You may not be on the level of notoriety as Target but that does not mean that you should treat yourself or your brand any less. You are just as David proclaimed in Psalm 139:14, "fearfully and wonderfully made." God's works are beautiful. If He gave you the assignment, it is beautiful. It is excellent. It is great. At this moment you may not be living in the full manifestation of the dream but know that it comes after faithful and consistent work. Your business deserves the respect that Target receives; however, it is tough to command something you do not believe. You teach people not to take you seriously when you do not show that you are serious through your actions.

My business began as a freelance gig while I was employed full-time as a college student. I was working in government and would take up small jobs on the side to make extra cash. Just a moment of honesty here, I had no idea the spirit of entrepreneurship was inside of me at this time. I've always been very creative and a hard worker so it seemed natural to take up opportunities to make more money using my gifts. Fast forward a couple of years and I was working in the private sector while still operating my business on the side. By this time I had a clearer direction for my firm and began to develop it even more. I incorporated the business, purchased my domain and began to make the steps so I couldn't operate it full-time. During this time I began to pray that God would allow me to get a "miracle contract" that would afford me to leave my job. It didn't happen that way. I was let go from my job and forced to make my business grow. Understand that God knows us enough to know when it's time for change. He will allow certain situations to happen because as much as we say, "Lord help me to _____," He knows that fear can keep us from moving to do the very thing we are praying to do. That's what God did for me in this situation. The very day I was let go I began to follow up on inquiries and respond to requests for proposals. I believed this was my moment. I knew this was the birthing of my nationally known firm. I wasn't there yet. There were no immediate results but I KNEW IT WAS COMING!

My loved ones saw me working and with love they would say, "Do you want to file for unemployment? Are you going to look for a job?" I knew was God spoke to me so I would tell them, "I'm not unemployed." My hard work prior to this had to be rewarded. It is the law of the land that you reap what you sow. I knew the seeds I planted. I knew what God was clearly speaking to me. Within two months I landed four contracts that not only paid my monthly expenses but exceeded what I was making when I was previously employed. Don't tell me what God won't do! Matthew 25:3 became real in my life during that time. I walked in what God showed me. I did not think of myself less. I knew who I was in God's eyes. I could not call myself a child of The King and not present work that is a reflection of royalty. It is not a spirit of arrogance. It is confidence. As sure as you are in the God that created you, His death, burial and resurrection, that should be your assurance in the gift that He gave you. Have you ever looked at the majestic work of the Universe? How amazing is it? How incredibly intricate is the human body and its ability to know what is wrong and send us signals? To create life? That's what God creates! He also created that invention that you have sitting in that notebook by the bed. He also created that ability you have to write and belt a song at a moments notice. He also created that ability you have to speak life into youth. That's what God creates! Isn't it beautiful? Why not treat it as so? Don't shortchange yourself and say "My business doesn't need all of that right now." You need that and more. Don't insult God's creation.

Take look these five keys I want to share with you to help you improve you maximize your online accessibility. On a weekly basis I am approached by entrepreneurs who want to enhance their social media presence. Statements like "Follow me on Twitter/Instagram" and "Like my Facebook Page" have become synonymous with passing a business card. The magic of social media does not happen simply by existing. Your business or brand will not grow just because you created your social accounts. After you have decided which social sites are best for you (that's another topic,) the following tips are sure to help you improve your social media and expand your brand!

CONSISTENCY

<u>Key questions about consistency</u>: *How often do you post material? Can your followers rely on you for regular posts? Do you have a plan for how often you post?*
If you can not respond with a resounding YES to each question then you must work on your consistency. Pick at least two or three days where you will share information on your pages. This will build your trust with your audience and they will begin to share your posts with their respective audiences.

CONTENT

<u>Key questions about content</u>: *What information are you sharing? Are you seen as an expert in your field? Do you have a plan for the content you post?*
You should have two goals related to the content you share:to be an industry expert and for your brand's personality to show through the content posted. Share informative articles, pop culture news and events related to your industry but you should also share funny YouTube or Vine videos. Avoid being one-dimensional in the content you share.

Be as diverse in your content as you would in a conversation at a social mixer with industry colleagues.

CONNECT

<u>Key questions about connecting</u>: *Do you respond to questions and comments? Do you encourage follower participation? Do you have a plan for connecting with your followers?*

One of the most damaging actions a brand can take online is not knowing how to connect with their followers. Your posts and graphics (even outside of online) should encourage social media sharing. Ask for your followers' opinions or feedback on the content you have shared. Be sure that every person on your team knows how to handle follower comments (good or bad.) Do not simply re-tweet positive comments while ignoring the negative ones. Engage your audience completely.

CREATIVITY

<u>Key questions about creativity</u>: *Is your logo or signature content shared? Are your graphics professionally designed? Do you have a plan for your creative material?*

Remove yourself from being the manager of your page and sincerely evaluate it. Ask a close friend if your social media presence is intriguing. Feel free to check out the pages of others who have large followings. Incorporate social media into your events. Create unique hash tags that invite users to engage with you. (This goes back to #3.)

CAPITALIZE

<u>Key questions about capitalizing</u>: *How do you acquire new followers? What makes them share content? What is your plan for capitalizing on your followers' demographics?*

Analytics... That's the name of the game! Find out where your followers live. Be conscious of that as you share content. Pay attention to posts that get abnormally high likes, shares and replies. Thank your followers to engaging and begin to share similar content more often.

Chapter Six

Early December of 2014 introduced the social media world, particularly Twitter, to a company by the name of Strange Fruit PR. Yes, Strange Fruit. (If you aren't sure why that's important have no fear. We will discuss it soon.) The nearly two year old firm was based in Austin, Texas and represented restaurants and other hospitality related brands. Let's pause and make sure everyone is on the same page with why the name is important in this discussion. In 1939 Bille Holiday released a song on the same title. It was a lyrical protest in reference to the lynchings taking place in the country. The lyrics, as written by Abel Meeropol, stated "Southern trees bear strange fruit, Blood on the leaves and blood at the root, Black bodies swinging in the southern breeze..." For many decades there was no other meaning or association with the words "strange fruit" other than the song made famous by the captivating Billie Holiday and the heaviness of the horror that it represented.

Back to the day when Twitter discovered this company existed. It is unclear who began the outcry against the name but it didn't take long for it to spread like wildfire. People began messaging the firm, contacting their clients, releasing information about the founders and calling for them to change their name. Many called for them to close their doors altogether. One could only wonder how a public relations firm made such an error. Initially it was assumed that they didn't know the meaning of the word and had just, in horrible decision making, failed to thoroughly research it. After all, one quick Google search would have introduce them to

71

the song. We discovered ignorance was not the case in this situation. The founders were aware of the history behind the name. The statements below are exact quotes from tweets posted from their @StrangeFruitPR account.

"Our passion is telling the stories of hospitality professionals. We chose our name bc [sic] these incredible talented artists stand out in a crowd

We believe in hospitality. Including all. No exclusion. The author & its famous singer hoped for a world where that would be a possibility.

Different is good. Cultivating an accepting, progressive community is good. We are proponents for all. Always have been. We wish you well."

If you are like me then you probably raised an eyebrow after reading those statements. It's clear they were aware of the meaning but felt like they could change the connotation that comes with the name. It's not the best idea to purposely use a name, statement or symbol that has a knowingly negative response. It becomes less about changing the perception and can be taken as disrespectful. That's exactly what happened in this situation. It was taken as blatant disregard and the public outcry continued well after the issued that statement.

I'm going to pause right here to point out how important social media posts are to your brand. A tweet, Facebook or Instagram post have the same relevance as a press conference. Be sure that you will have no issues sticking by the statement once your emotion is gone. Celebrities and public figures have been known to delete a regretful post after the response was less than favorable. Avoid that by making sure that everything you post is levelheaded, clear and something you want to represent your brand. Remember, people judge you by your online presence.

Back to the team at Strange Fruit PR. After they issued those statements via Twitter they still found themselves in a public relations crisis. Oh, the irony. After much consideration they decided they would change the name of their company to Perennial PR. It would seem that this would be done with the utmost care, considering what they had just experienced. Not quite. They issued a press release announcing the name prior to securing the social media accounts attributed to the new name. Someone in internet land took it upon themselves to make @PerennialPR a satire account. Yes, the nightmare continued. They made fun of the company's owners, made disparaging remarks and taught the "public relations representatives" a few lessons about protecting your image. A situation that should have gone away quickly, thanks to the public's short attention span, gained an additional 15 minutes of fame.

There are so many issues within this situation so let's unpack each one and discuss a few tips. Before you attempt to incorporate or announce a name or even a new slogan for your brand, research it. Enter it in the search engine and see what comes up. I have experienced situations where a client will want to use a commonly known name or motto in tandem with their own but "put their spin on it." Be careful with that. In most situations I recommend staying away from those types of situations. Not only can you flirt with the line of copyright infringement, but you can risk dealing with the headache of confusing the audience about who you are. When you build your identity based on something someone else has used, the message becomes confusing.

Think of this example for a moment. You are tasked with being substitute teacher for a day. The dry erase board has writing all over it and there is no eraser in sight. You attempt to erase it with a napkin but realize the messages were written in permanent marker. You try to write your name in a free white space but it gets lost in the chaos. You are very clear on where you placed your name but it does not stand out. The message that was there before you put your stamp on it continues to dominate the board.

That's what happens when you take a name with a known historical or cultural meaning and make it your own. I am not saying it's impossible but I am saying it's probably not worth the work. If you feel like recycling a name is your only resort then I would encourage you to continue searching for a name. Go back to your focus group and test names and slogans on them before putting it out. Get their feedback or even their suggestions. Don't get so stuck on the first name that hit you that it prevents you from accepting feedback on it.

The next step in the naming process is securing the necessary brand protection before publicly announcing it. Purchase your web domain. Open your social media accounts. File for your copyright, trademark or patent. How tragic would it be to go through the work to establish an identity only to have someone snatch away the rewards because you didn't protect yourself?! Also, use wisdom with sharing your information. Have your focus groups sign release forms. Consult with an attorney about the best way to protect yourself in these situations.

The name of your business or brand should not be extremely complicated. I understand that the goal is to have something unique. Do not go so far in the deep end that you come up with a name that only makes sense to you and is difficult to regurgitate. There's a fine line between being different and being complicated. You don't want your difference to become a detraction because it's just too much to handle. Yes, this is your business but if your customers are not happy, you have no business.

SECTION FOUR

It's YOUR responsibility!!

Chapter Seven

"Walk with the wise and become wise, for a companion of fools suffers harm."
Proverbs 13:20, NIV

As the old adage goes, "Show me your friends and I will show you your future." Our circle of influence has an effect on the success of our brand. We can increase or decrease our brand's validity by our associations. I am sure you can think of several famous people who became well-known by being _____'s friend. You must be careful when adding members to your team. Your employees and volunteers are an extension of you and they represent who you are. They instantly become _____'s employee. That Facebook post, Instagram picture or blog post was done by _____'s employee. Be sure that you know who you are hiring to work with you. As a small business, you should still invest in the background check process necessary to know any and all alarming details about your employees. Search their social network activity. Be in the know!

SHARE THE VISION

Once you have built your team it is your responsibility to grow it. No one else has this task. You hold the vision and direction for your brand. Take time to share the future goals of the company along with the history. Talk to them about why you have made certain decisions. Include them in the process. I am not saying that they are empowered to make or influence your decisions; however, they should feel like they are a part on the company and not an employee or outsider. A few chapters ago we talked about how Chik-fil-A and McDonald's were able to get their partner teams to buy into their philosophies. It is essential! It is not your team's fault if they don't know how to or fail to accurately represent your brand. As the leader, the vision and energy flows from you. If you approach your project with excitement on a level four, don't be surprised when you receive a level two in return. Your job is not to be what you want them to be. You have to be greater than you want them to be. Take time with your team members! Pay attention to them and develop their skills. Empower them to be problem solvers instead of problem proclaimers. Anyone can point out a problem but it's a blessing to have someone who fixes a problem.

I have been in employment situations where I was both empowered to solve a problem and crippled from finding a solution. My productivity in the former situation was much higher. I did not rebel in the latter circumstance. The difference was that my environment encouraged creativity so I was able to do more on my job. I found new ways to get things done and even created new practices. That's the type of culture you want to built. When the team is on one page and is happy, the customers will know.

Publix has a reputation for fostering a positive grocery shopping experience. They truly live up to their motto, "Where shopping is a pleasure." I often find myself going out of my way and spending a few more dollars to shop at Publix. I'm not the only person who does that either. A pleasant environment with quality products will always guarantee that your customers are not just consumers but they are now promoters. They become your unofficial street team and encourage others to be customers of yours as well.

That type of energy does not start from the outside. It cannot happen if there is strife or micromanagement happening within the team. Share your core values. Engage them in team building exercises. Find out their strengths. Lead by your actions. Your team is one of the most valuable parts of building your brand. You can have the best graphics, website, building, product and marketing plan. It all fails if your team is not involved in or does not support it.

Chapter Eight

I created this manual for the go-getter. The person who is constantly on-the-go, trying to figure it all and make it happen. The one who feels like they are constantly working against the clock. This is just the first volume.. I hope these tips were helpful! There are so many other keys to building a successful brand but God said for me to stop here. (That was SO hard to accept.)

See you at the top but if you ever need my help along the way, know that I am here for you!

Acknowledgments

I could never thank God enough for gifting me with this vision and seeing it through. Mommy, there is no another woman like you on earth! I strive to have the impact you have on people. I am so grateful to you and Dad for your undying support through this process. Nikki, Martin, Elsie, Joshua and Jacob, I am honored to be your sister. You guys consistently push me to be a better person. Thank you for loving me. Latecia and Jasmine, blood couldn't make us closer. You guys "know where the bodies are buried" and you've never tried to use that against me. Through the good, bad and ugly your friendship has remained consistent. Brittany B., you are the best right hand ever!!

I'm afraid to call names here so I will use words that these groups know. I could not have done this without OUO, MB #5 and 434. You are the epitome of real friends!

To Bishop and Lady McKissick, Jr., Bishop and Lady McKissick, Sr. and my entire Bethel family, thank you for your support. Bishop McKissick, Jr., I am so grateful for your collaboration on this project. It's such an honor.

My life became better the day I connected with my best friend. He deserves co-author credit, especially since he named the book. He is truly the reflection of God's love for me and I am forever thankful for his love, support, encouragement and motivation. Desmond, I appreciate and love you forever! We did it!

To every friend, loved one, acquaintance, colleague, mentor and client, know that I appreciate you. This is only the beginning. The next level awaits us!

www.ingramcontent.com/pod-product-compliance
Lightning Source LLC
Chambersburg PA
CBHW071117210326
41519CB00020B/6326